Was sie sieht | What she sees

Sarah Elizabeth Moreman

Presentation by *BookLeaf Publishing*

Web: www.bookleafpub.com

E-mail: info@bookleafpub.com

ISBN: 9789358735604

First edition 2023

ACKNOWLEDGEMENT

Only the Creator can see what the future holds, and He knew what He was doing with this little girl who held sunshine in her smile.

To my parents who did not take the well-grooved path of raising their baby who was born profoundly bisensorineural deaf. Instead, they researched all possible options before meeting the founder of the Cued Speech, Dr. Orin Cornett.

Growing up with a sibling who has hearing impairment could not have been straightforward. Yet my three siblings, Hank, Brad, and Josie, took it all in stride and would not let me feel any different. "You were our experience just like we were your experience."

To Aunt Glen, who skillfully cross-stitched lovely designs onto the pockets that my mother customized to hold my body-worn hearing aid box when wearing my dresses.

To Kate Daisy, whom I also call as MyBaby, for having nicknamed Cued Speech as "chin-ano" and coaching me through the self-choreographed renditions to the "Somewhere Out There" song by singers Linda Ronstadt and James Ingram for the soundtrack of the animated feature film titled *An American Tail* (1986).

To my soul sister, Beth, who took me to her dance class at Love Dance Academy, opening my eyes about taking dance classes, which resulted in thirteen years at Nix Dance Studios.

To my tall blonde warrioress, Deborah Strawn, for being who she is and for being there for me for four decades and counting.

To all my ten transliterators, heartfelt thanks for being with me, making sure I get all the information in each and every academic class, plus teaching me about life from your respective perspectives—Kim Austin, Debbie Wade, Shelley McLaughlin Rohwer, DeAnna McKnight Angle, Katy Crum, Tamara Massey, Sherylyn Ware Smith, Ginger Wheat Key, Lara Peel, and Tom Hilyer.

PREFACE

Trust in the Lord with all your heart,
and lean *NOT* on your own understanding;
in all your ways acknowledge Him,
and He shall direct your paths.
— Proverbs 3:5-6 (NKJV)

Then, looking up to heaven, He sighed
and said to him, "Ephphatha,"
that is, "Be opened."
Immediately his ears were opened,
and the impediment of his tongue
was loosed, and he spoke plainly.
...He even makes the deaf hear.
— Mark 7:34-35, 37 (NKJV)

"Was sie sieht" is German for "what she sees".

Born profoundly bisensorineural deaf, the author shares how having hearing impairment instills within her a strong sense of discernment. From wearing the body hearing aids to wearing behind-the-ear (BTE) digital hearing aids well into her late thirties, Dr. Moreman's perspective is more visual than auditory.

What she sees enhances her hearing comprehension.

Yet over time, she learns to go beyond what she sees by going deeper in faith rather than by sight. In her autoethnographic dissertation, Dr. Moreman created a chapter titled "See the Writing" kaleidoscopic lens to share vignettes of her experiences on her journey to becoming a college teacher. Therefore, Dr. Moreman invites others to catch a glimpse through her kaleidoscopic lens as she grew up experiencing the world with hearing impairment.

In this autobiographical collection of poems, Dr. Moreman uses poetic license when sharing particular vivid details to evoke a sense of belonging and storytelling.

Reaching for the sunshine
of sound

Reaching into awareness,
parallel to reaching light at the end
of Plato's cave,
I smile as my hands grab ahold of the knee,
laughing as the leg swings me,
giving me a joy ride.

Reveling in the swings of joy
under the sun rays of smiles shining upon my
raised countenance, feeling the
glow in my chest.

Every experience framed as vignette
as a curved-corner photo from the
nineteen-eighties,
the negatives in sepia tone showing
smiles as apparitions glowing

Ensconced in love and security,
I do not know pain, indifference, or even evil.
I only know different levels of brightness in love
some of contentment
some of cheerfulness
some of combusting sparks

Fingering the tightly twisted thin wires
leading from the brown box nestling
inside my chest pocket
to my ears

Amplification gives me sound,
making me smile and laugh more

Kinderprep

Long dark mirrors covering walls,
low, long tables the color of sand,
fluorescent lighting distracting
from high ceilings,
paper covered with crayon
scribblings and stick figures

A boy with glasses
sitting in his wheelchair
with his mouth open, appearing as if
he is laughing and talking at the same time,
his crooked hand struggling to hold the fruit

I tug at a nearby grown-up's pants, pulling
the fabric covering the knee
to come closer. She kneels and I point,
"Orange is orange!"
She smiles and repeats with me,
"Orange is orange."

The boy hears us, his open mouth
widening into a bigger smile

Across the table, big pouty lips
with a bit of tongue sticking out
her half-moon eyes
twinkling and bubbling with giddiness
as she waves at me. I wave back
even though our toes are touching
and kicking, playing tag

When we move to the floor,
many pictures capturing moments
of playtime or story time,
one black and white photo in the newspaper
of our smiling faces glued together
side by side,
capturing the joys of the program
designed by my warrioress

Looking up to my tall blue-eyed warrioress,
admiring her long blonde hair
while she gives undivided attention
to each and every one of us.
She is my patient, content warrioress
who listens to my jibber jabber

Kindred challenge with one girl
only a year older and has a younger sister,
both on the next level of hearing cognition,
where my stubbornness keeps reaching
and not yet reaching

Two role models, one being my brother.
I am glad he is with me.
—he looks out for me, I look at him for clues.
He is regular, nothing out of ordinary,
yet a measure for us to understand life
and how we can hone what we do have.

Traversing the rooftop of Haley Center,
squinting eyes under the brightness of the sun
seeing the chalk in different colors,
mostly white lines and dotted yellow lines
some green or red signs

Individuals or in groups
navigate the chalked traffic layout,
some walk, some ride tricycles, some stand
mostly within white lines

My pink sneakers on the pedals
of a low-slung Cabbage Patch Kid tricycle,
my hands gripping the handlebars
with plastic white-mint green ribbons,
my eagerness to go fast
I wanna go fast
only I must stop at the corners with
the red chalk of eight-sided signs

Some hold hands to cross streets,
my warrioress holds the hand of the one
who cannot see, helping her to cross the street

Watching the movement of others…
watching the little world we are shaping
with our own application of understanding
to survive out there in the bigger world

My hands gripping the handlebars,
my pink sneakers on the pedals,
my breathing rhyming with anticipation,
looking at my role models
looking at my blonde warrioress
for clues

Auburn University Kinderprep program
1982-1985
established by Deborah Strawn,
my tall blonde warrioress

falling with autumn leaves

autumn of water oak leaves
bringing the smoky crisp smells of exuberance,
their colors of burnt orange
and golden eagle brown
covering the grassy meadow,
nestling underneath the water oak

following Brad in his red and blue puff vest,
jumping into mounds of water oak leaves
reveling in the crackling and rustling
as I sink deeper to feel underneath
the hard cold damp grass

golden beacon of the setting sun
shining through the branches still graced
with water oak leaves waiting to dance
to the ground, the sky deepening
its vibrant blueness into navy

reveling in the crackling and rustling
of the water oak leaves, a breeze
tiptoeing its cool toes along my exposed
neck underneath the puff vest that matches
my brother's

Pam with her winged hair of the eighties
her dark pea coat and brown gloves
exuding smartness as she held up her
rectangular Pentax to capture our laughter
mingling with the crackling and rustling

an afternoon of simplicity with Pam
captured in memorable photos
stored in a doll's chest of drawers
among plastic aqua bead necklaces,
pink combs, and warped fun mirrors

I pull out to see and remember
how someone from the University
wanted to spend an afternoon with Brad and me,
an afternoon falling with autumn leaves
crackling, rustling, laughing, sun shining

remembering how I did not want
the afternoon with Pam to end,
waving as she slowly drove away
down the long gravel driveway
lined with pecan trees

Auburn, Alabama
Grammy's backyard
Autumn 1984

rustling amplification

rustling as the fabric grazes
over the tight thin wires
connecting the box at the chest
to the earmolds

rustling prickles across
the nerves, making my teeth
want to bite down on the wires
and earmolds

rustling startles the
nerves into embracing life
rustling reminding me
to adjust, to situate better

rustling a comfort
as my hair pulled back
into a ponytail,
yet sometimes irritating

rustling irritation of whine that draws
forth others' alarmed expressions
my reassuring them
—not a ticking bomb

rustling when hugging
friends embracing
this trademark of hugging,
the whine for them

rustling brushes across
my consciousness, electrifying
my synapses when pulling
my hair into a ballerina's bun

rustling amplification
rubbing and scratching the mesh wire
of a microphone, calling me
to speak and share

residual hearing

although born profoundly
bisensorineural deaf,
residual hearing exists

similar to shades of skin tone,
shades of hearing loss

deaf as a doornail, dead deaf, nothing
profound hearing loss, no phone
severe hearing loss, yes phone
hard of hearing, can fool us
circumstantial, aging hearing loss,
unwilling to admit or wear hearing aids
normal hearing, regular

residual hearing exists,
occasionally surprising others,
thus easier to explain with volume
rather than with frequencies

amplify residual hearing
the minute I was given
that box, I fell in love with sound

I refused letting anyone
take the box off, not willing
to let the sound go

my mother sewing pockets
my aunt cross-stitching
simply for that box, allowing
me to run after my brothers

I nurtured the residual hearing
by wearing that box constantly,
even in my fuchsia-trimmed,
teal-colored bathing suit

graduated into hearing aids,
losing the box, yet refused wearing
the loop, since I stubbornly believed
in hearing aids being enough,
like Leslie, bargained with Deborah
must make all As to show
I did not need the loop

however, however
the FM system would have helped
me use more of my residual hearing,
captivating my awareness,
better comprehending my learning

yet chose the hard way
wanting own independence
in a less conspicuous way
wanting to be normal

analog vamped into digital
cassette tapes into CDs and DVDs
then again, into Blu-rays and clouds

the difference in sound quality
described as coming
out from behind the clouds,
or poking to the core of a balloon

steadfast in my stubbornness
wanting own independence
in a less conspicuous way
wanting to be normal

yet be natural, therefore
the why for refusal of the surgery,
wanting to be normal
yet be natural

residual hearing is natural
and the fear of losing the
natural sounds from residual hearing
prevailed for decades,
never mind the vanity

natural sounds, natural hearing
wondrously obtained even underwater
without wearing hearing aids,
could hear the shouts and laughter
reverberating in the air
while I held my breath, then slowly letting
out bubbles as I swam to the surface

why should I change the way
God has blessed me? He gave me
enough hearing yet gave me much more
with awareness and listening

Cued Speech

A hand movement
representing phonemes
transliteration

Not interpretation
Not sign language
Not even at all

MyBaby cousin birthing
the nickname of chin-ano
                    —piano and chin

Transliteration, a relay
of message to receiver

lipreading enhancement
listening engagement
looking enchantment

rhythmic blur of blending
the words into comprehension

instilling within me
awareness of residual hearing
and how to use it

instilling within me
the stubbornness
and wanting to be independent

the sensation of training wheels
coming off the bicycle
as I pedal faster

yet I look back with gratitude,
the foundation for communication
comprehensive and approachable

ten transliterators

Cued Speech, a hand movement
representing the phonemes of
sounds—may take one or two days
to learn, yet many more to practice

a keyboard or typewriter to blend
together letters into words, into paragraphs,
even the entire lecture, speech, or movie

fluidity from transliterator to next
smooth as I went from grade level to next

kindergarten was all mine, enforcing
my bullheadedness as I went mainstream
with only one superpower hour down the hall

first and second grades with Ms. Kim
and her sharp dress of dark fuchsia
dark enough to be purple,
her swift bringing me up to par with my peers,
making sure I pace in cadence

moved back to the
Loveliest Village on the Plains
honing my fierce independent spirit

adjusting to writing and third grade
with Ms. Debbie
and her pastel-colored legal pads,
love for country style with white geese

fourth grade to first half of sixth grade,
becoming a lady of poise,
started dancing,
dealing with discovery of boys
while riding the bus,
reading Nancy Drew and Hardy Boys,
while learning from gold-tressed Shelley,
ending with a floral crown as her junior
bridesmaid

second half of sixth grade,
ending with seventh grade
grew up faster in math, earned that top score
as Dee shared her brilliance and connections,
growing into public speaking the more I wrote
and understood my place

eighth grade split with Katy cheering me on
taking notes for me to master Algebra
while the leaves are falling,
ushering in the promise of spring
with Tamara and her Cher essence

first two years of high school
sparked in scholarship and perseverance
with Sheryl and her soul-stirring guidance
prodding me to reach beyond expectation,
continued guiding me and my peers
in the last two

the junior year became more personable
as Ginger stepped in,
expanding her youth group
leadership to be with me
five more days each week,
teaching me how to comprehend
the periodic table,
excelled Chemistry with a hundred
thanks to her,
subsequently gifted with an irreplaceable
friend in her younger sister Jane

the senior year became even more personable
as Lara stepped in,
only five years apart,
our bond strengthened, yet I wanted more
independence, a catalyst for the future
when I must grow up

Camp War Eagle when I met Tom
when I realized my bullheaded tendency
for independence, asking for different
accommodations to take the
spotlight off me and more on the professor

Ten transliterators—
transliteration
transformed
into transcription.

Twelve years with ten different transliterators:

Vaughn Road Elementary School, 1986-1988
Dean Road Elementary School, 1988-1990
Drake Middle School, 1990-1992
Auburn Junior High School, 1992-1994
Auburn High School, 1994-1998
Auburn University, Fall 1998

a princess between many worlds and her chauffeur

Seeing my brothers slipping out
past the screened metal porch door,
leaving for school on their bikes,
seeing my sister still sleeping
while I pull on my white top
and pink bottoms

Dad already gone for work,
Mom greeting me in the kitchen,
watching her cue "Good morning,"
eating my bowl of cereal,
watching through the window,
waiting for the dark navy vehicle

Pushing open the heavy kitchen door
out into the alley driveway
between the barracks,
he waiting for me, the door open
climbing into dark navy vehicle,
tugging on the seat belt,
the red-trimmed Strawberry Shortcake
metal lunch box across my knees

Quietly looking at Mr. Wes
as he smiled over his shoulder,
"Good morning, Miss Sarah"

Focusing on the pull of the vehicle
as he drove,
letting the dreams waft
through my mind,
watching the clouds and trees
pass by like a river,
letting my own world
blossom from the dreams

Feeling the vehicle sliding to a stop,
I pull on the handle before turning
to face Mr. Wes, saying "Thank you"

Pushing through one
of the many glass doors,
concentrating on the
brownish square tiles under my feet,
feeling the coolness from
the painted concrete block walls,
waking up to the echoes
from the surrounding clamor
of peers of all colors around my age

The day blurs by,
full of thin carpet, pencils, desks,
red-blue cushioned threefold mats,
sighs, whispers, and giggles filling the air,
foldable lunch tables, trays laden
with rectangle pizza and chocolate milk,

one hour set apart from the mainstream,
a long walk down the hallway
to be with others not part of the mainstream.
One hour and still not part of them,
must work more to participate
in the reward chart system,
to see those metallic star stickers
of any color next to my name
on the black marker-lined poster,
to be part of them, to learn some signs,
to interact and connect with them
albeit only for one hour…is the fuss worth it?

—one shining moment…
wearing that translucent yellow cape
I see myself as Snow White.
A show and tell march,
with the mainstream class,
from classroom to next classroom.
Entering the classroom of
my daily one hour out of mainstream,

one boy excited, saluting a fist at his shoulder,
signing, and pointing, "There's Sarah! There's
Sarah!"

Wondering at his and others' excitement of
seeing me
as I follow mainstream out of that classroom—

Pondering that one shining moment many a time
on the long walk down the hallway after
the one superpower hour ends,
switching back to mainstream,
reacquainting myself, resituating myself,
picking up a freshly sharpened pencil,
writing my name and filling in worksheets,
lining up for P.E. and the coach
wearing a whistle,
its high pitch out of my range,
running together in circles on dry grass,
climbing huge tractor tires, monkey bars,
back to desks, whispers, and writing
before picking up backpacks

Waving others bye as I walk back alone
to the many glass doors, choosing one to open,
stepping out in the sun, onto the sidewalk

The navy vehicle already at the curb,
he waiting for me, the door open
Climbing inside, taking in
the car leather smells,
tugging on the seat belt,
pulling the metal lunch box across my knees,
my backpack as my double cushion

Quietly looking at Mr. Wes
as he smiled over his shoulder,
"Ready to go home, Miss Sarah?"

Montgomery, Alabama
Vaughn Road Elementary School,
Kindergarten to Second Grade, 1985-1988

the treehouse moments

a bunk bed fashioned into a treehouse
in Mrs. Richburg's third grade classroom

treehouses of our childhood
filled with imagination and promises
places of escape, reading, and learning

    ...or I thought so when
    she said something
    I did not understand

But at the base of the treehouse,
shocked expressions of our homeroom
teacher and classmates told me
the insinuation of her words

I still think about that treehouse moment
and wondered what she said.

However, we grew up together
in good stead and enjoyed camaraderie.
She was and still is a good friend.
She grew out of whatever she said.

Still seeing in my mind
those shocked expressions
of our homeroom teacher and classmates,
I wondered if others remembered
what she said

The treehouse moment is one of many
where I did not catch what the other person
said, but I did catch the reactions of others
surrounding us

The treehouse moments of thoughtless,
impulsive, bold, even rude words
revealing the sayer's innermost regard
and thoughts

The treehouse moments are for us
to exercise the faith of forgiving,
trusting that the sayer would reflect
on the spoken words later

The treehouse moments are for us
to wonder at the imagination of such words,
to forgive the broken childhood innocence
and sense of belonging

The treehouse moments are not for us
to fall through the splintering wood
of poorly constructed words, instead to perch
on the good planks of proactive forgiveness

The treehouse moments are still there
for imaginations and promises to be rebuilt
with better constructed words
and patience

Auburn, Alabama
Dean Road Elementary School,
Third Grade, 1988-1989

facial cues

seeing a smile welcomes,
stepping forward into the circle,
natural breathing with
subconscious confidence,
returning a smile of my own

seeing a frown forbids,
stepping backwards from the circle,
forcing myself to remember
how to breathe,
keeping my face composed

seeing the friendliness in the eyes,
stepping forward into the circle,
my heart in good, hopeful rhythm
opening my mouth, confident
in connecting

seeing the dismay in the eyes,
stepping further away from the circle,
my heart twisting in irregular rhythm
thinning my lips, insecure
in connecting

seeing the lips move to ask or invite,
I respond with gladness, understanding
that I will be understood,
willing to listen
and being

Seeing the lips turn upside down
in confusion or accusation,
I respond with dread, understanding
that I will not be understood,
making an effort to appease

Break the circle, bend
both the pleasant and not so pleasant
together into a strong infinity
of seeking to understand
rather than to be understood.

Life is more than insisting
Life is about communicating
Life is about comprehending
Life is about relating, connecting
Life is about giving grace

Expecting to be understood
creates more angst,
Seeking to understand
creates more grace
—communicating is an art…

Taking responsibility to communicate
means to put aside wants and needs
and focus on the other,
to absorb the moment
rather than insisting

Words artfully constructed,
framed and decorated
with body language and
face.

The face shows more
than the words.

longing to be normal

Harsh brilliance of the glaring sun
Sweat droplets sliding down skin
Field day is a field day
All day full of games
Water and bathroom breaks
the only respite

Many girls wearing ponytails
I refuse to wear a ponytail
no matter how drenched
somebody offers an elastic
shaking my head no
I move into position to run

Slapping hands with teammate,
I take off, running across the field
feeling the wind rushing through
my long caramel hair, the baby fine
strands of white gold pulling gently
from the hairline

Running faster, returning to my team
before even slowing to a halt, my hand
reaches up to smooth down my
wind-whipped hair into place
over my ears,
where the hearing aids sit

a story of the babysitter's conviction

The first ten months of my life
Something seemed mysterious about me
      The happiest baby anyone has ever seen
Yet something seemed mysterious about me

Doctors checked and gave tests
many possible diagnoses discussed
      deafness not even considered though
      Something seemed not right

Back and forth, more tests given
More possible diagnoses uncertain
      All the while, I was one happy baby
      A portrait of contentment

Anyone could easily put me in the corner
and I would not make a fuss
      Rather, I glowed happy
      making everyone smile

I hardly ever cried,
yet something seemed mysterious about me
      Should we be concerned?
      The happiest baby anyone has ever seen

It was ten months later
when the snow piled up, packing it thick
Christmas lights making the streets twinkle
as my parents left for a gathering

The babysitter checked to make sure
I was my usual happy self in the corner
and that my brothers were behaving
before she started washing dishes

Soap and hot water in the sink
so fixated on the heavenliness of cleaning
that a pot slipped out of her hand
and clanged loud,

                    a heavy thud

Something seemed mysterious about me
                    for I did not cry out

The dread the babysitter felt
as she came up behind me,
clapping her hands,
calling my name
                    No response
Holding her breath, she slowly
        maneuvered into my peripheral vision
and clapped, saying my name

Seeing her, I looked up at her
and smiled, laughed with joy
          The dread the babysitter felt
                    stung

                              deeper

She waited until Sunday morning,
two days afterwards, the day of the Lord
once the last hymn was sung,
flame from the Advent candles flickered,
conviction pulling the babysitter
down the aisle, to my parents' pew

She leaned in as to whisper,
          "You may want to have
                    her hearing checked."
My parents appreciated her.

The next morning saw me bundled
up in knitted wool blankets and took me
back to the same doctor who initially
had not considered deafness

Tests ran, and the diagnosis
          solved the mystery.

December 1980

daddy's ballerina after all

once the diagnosis has been confirmed,
what would my parents do?
       No family history of hearing loss

They *already* thought
I was special, because
       I was the first girl

My two brothers were looking
forward to having a baby sister
       —The first girl

My father thought
this first girl would be
       his ballerina

once the diagnosis was confirmed,
       would the dream of his little girl
       becoming a ballerina ever come true?

My parents agonized
about how to raise their little girl

They must consider
       communication, family, and education

My mother went out for a walk
As snow crunched under her boots,
          her heart grew lighter as her eyes lifted

The sky dark and yet shimmery,
twinkling with ice cold diamonds of stars,
          beyond which she saw blessings

Walking back, more like skipping,
her heart now content, knowing that
          God has a purpose for this child—me

Eight years later, I came home,
after watching Beth's dance class,
          declaring, "I want to dance."

Sweeping my hair up

Sweeping my hair up
only for practice, for the stage
jetés, assemblés, and sautés
across the hardwoods
on which anchored with resin
when en pointe

keeping in rhythm with my peers
the hardest for me
as I rely on my eyes,
—not any sound

no such thing as feeling vibrations
on the hardwood
as I relevé and en pointe,
'tis the same as feeling the air
—imaginative

I focus on keeping in rhythm
with my peers, always
a second or two behind

sweeping my hair up
only for practice, for the stage
as I rely on my eyes

to see fluidity in the air,
...not in the melody
...not in the music

When in mesmerizing trance,
what I see is more from the heart,
when finally warming up,
into the rhythm of the dance

Allowing myself to loosen up,
not thinking about how I looked
as my heart leads my body
to align with the music

Letting myself free
as my lips curved into a smile,
The lights caressing the aura
of my chaînés and pirouettes

Auburn, Alabama
Love Dance Academy, 1988-1989
Nix Dance Studios, 1989-2001

Seeing Miss America 1995

Her artistic dance to Via Dolorosa
white gown in stated elegance
glittering already with inspiration
before being crowned Miss America

Before she graced the stage,
    I was already dancing

Before she graced the stage,
    I was already speaking

Before she graced the stage,
    my grasp of life
    was already blossoming

Yet I was drawn to emulate
the grace through dancing
the compelling through speaking
the being growing from faith

Standing before her,
not knowing where to begin,
not wanting to leave before
understanding beyond

Understanding beyond
the public perception,
        wanting to know something
        no one else knew, not even her family

My raw question about having friends
revealing the need for connection,
        in her dark eyes, immediate recognition
        beyond the raw question

Her diplomatic response
held hidden layers of meaning
        only a blessed few understood
        beyond the public perception

We met again over lunch
a decade later,
        yet I kept quiet,
        not asking another raw question

The divergence began
with her diplomatic response,
        the hidden layers of meaning
        she and I silently understood

First meeting at Auburn University
January 1995

Second meeting at Olive Garden,
Montgomery, Alabama
January 2005

Miss Teen of Auburn

Designing my choreography
with my cousin as my ears,
timing "Somewhere Out There"
as I watch her coaching my steps

Stuffing my bag with costumes
and pointe shoes, garment bag
with formal gowns, my courage
in expression of self-choreography

Flying across the country
seeing my face among thousands
on the welcoming wall
meeting others

the first gathering, the blue ribbon the focus
on making a difference, Helice seeing me,
her walking up the steps, stopping at the row
where I sit, motioning for me to join her

Among thousands, she has seen me
I wonder as I join her on the
platform, my cheeks feeling warm
I see her continue her speech

About making a difference
what the blue ribbon signifies,
then she pauses before
declaring who I am

Not sure why or how she knows
about me, I straighten my spine,
lifting my chin before seeing
the faces of my fellow competitors

Helice smiling at me, then turning
her gaze back at the audience, declaring
her own good news about Broadway,
I gasp as the audience cheers

Not knowing a single soul,
and she picks me among thousands
to share the moment with her,
because she sees the blue ribbon in me

That blue ribbon moment carries
me throughout the week as others
include me in their moments,
welcoming me

The practice reveals flaws,
shoving me into frantic
improvisations, keeping the teachings
of the dance studio and my cousin

The blue ribbon moment
reminds me of courage as I perform
en pointe to my self-choreographed
rendition of "Somewhere Out There"

Miss Teen of America Scholarship Program
San Diego, California
July 1996

the enigma of talking
on the phone

my mother came home, looking solemn
a tear or two in her eyes,
asking me why did i answer the phone,
explaining that a child should not tell
whoever it was on the other end
that the parents were not home

i answered the phone, thinking
i would find the magic of being normal,
if i could only make sense of the syllables,
the jumbled syllables and inflections

looking at my mother's face,
resigning that i would not get to find
that magic of being normal

seeing Hank wind the long twisted
telephone cord around the doorjamb,
scratching the paint off the wood,
leaving grooves

listening to my brother's voice,
noting the low and high pitches
of the syllables, not deciphering

what he was saying, and he talked
and talked for hours, the intonation,
learning to pick up on the inflection
in his voice

intuiting my curiosity,
my blonde warrioress arranged,
appeasing my curiosity

placing these phones on the table
before me at school, set up as practice,
my blonde warrioress teaching me
the value of the FM system,
concentrating hard to listen,
recognizing the words on paper
in front of me that match what i heard,
responding with confidence

opening my eyes through these phone
practices, recognizing that send-off tone
of "Okay, talk to you later. Bye."
or "Love you. Bye."

seeing through listening the cadence
of others speaking through their phones,
the modulation of their voices,
the mechanical, distorted intonation
the grainy, static noise visualized
as the retro television screen,

yet the sharp precision of Matrix
punctuated with distinctive syllables,
waiting for that send-off tone,
never failing to make me feel
solid and encouraged, connected

always listening for that send-off tone,
a sense of familiarity, along with
typical everyday phrases such as
"What time is it?"
"Time to eat"
"Let's go"

the inflection
the syllables
the punctuation
the expected words
i recognize and embrace

the soundproof booth

sitting at the table, visual aid
charts spread out on the surface,
seeing the audiologist and
graduate students scribbling
in their legal pads

seeing them whisper,
absorbing their whispers,
watching their body language,
waiting for the next step,
seeing them stand up,
one motioning me to follow

swinging open the heavy,
double-door design of metal,
seeing the acoustic walls,
sitting and leaning back in the chair,
watching the grad student
fumbling the listening devices,
clipping them on my shirt,
handing me the clicker,
telling me to click
if I hear anything

at my assenting nod,
fluid movement of the grad student
accompanies the door swinging out,
cooler air seeping in,
the grad student slipping out,
the sensation of a vacuum,
the door trapping me inside,
latching shut,
its magnetic seal preventing
sound leakage

wriggling my fingers while
gripping the clicker,
my eyes taking in the
movements of the audiologists
beyond the window,
the silence bearing down on my bones,
breathing in a controlled way
as to not make the silence louder,
skimming my eyes on the black dots
in the soundproof metal walls,
the black dots exuding strong
presence of silence,
dulling my brain, lethargy
evading my conscious

waiting to receive the occasional
breaks in the deafening silence,
anticipating for those breaks of

lethargy
come on! Send those beeps,
break the lethargy,
break the deafening silence

not wanting to guess,
not wanting to predict,
not wanting to mess up,
willing for my hearing
willing to improve
willing to impress
willing for the wow results

♦ ♦ ♦ beeep — beeeoooop ♦ ♦ ♦

Exhaling the long-held breath,
dispelling the grips of
deafening silence and its power
of lethargy

Lowering my eyes to the clicker
in my grip, not willing to look
through the window, to see
what they are doing, to see
their body language,
otherwise it feels like cheating
like standing on tiptoes when
my dad measured my growing height

♦ ♦ ♦ beeep — beeep — beeep ♦ ♦ ♦

watching the base of my thumbnail
turn white while pressing the button
on the clicker in my grip, my shoulders
relaxing

keep the beeps coming,
keep the deafening silence away,
keep the lethargy away

♦ ♦ ♦ whrrrp — whrrrp ♦ ♦ ♦

♦ ♦ ♦ chrrrp — cheep-cheep ♦ ♦ ♦

♦ ♦ ♦ hiss — hisssssssssss ♦ ♦ ♦

♦ ♦ ♦ whoob — whooob — whooo ♦ ♦ ♦

♦ ♦ ♦ buzzzz — buzzzzzzzzz ♦ ♦ ♦

♦ ♦ ♦ shhhhhhh ♦ ♦ ♦

♦ ♦ ♦ ping ♦ ♦ ♦

A movement on the other side
of the window
of someone standing up
catching my downcast eyes,

my thumb relaxing from hovering
over the button on the clicker
pandemonium revival

onomatopoeic sound of latching open
double-door swinging open,
cooler air rushing in,
seeping into my tired bones,
reviving me from the lethargy,
from the deafening silence

the listening devices unclipped
from my shirt, the corners of my mouth
lifting up into a smile
breathing more naturally
pandemonium revival

gliding back in the seat
at the table with the audiologists,
learning that my hearing
remains the same as always
with my own unique map
of frequencies,
yet praised for using my
residual hearing well,
thus maintaining a healthy
synaptic connection between
hearing and brain

the deaf stare

wearing the green-striped sunflower dress,
weaving dandelions into wreaths,
weaving smiles into joy

yet when i need to focus,
the look of concentration
freezes my face into slack wonder

the deaf stare

I cringe when I catch myself
wearing the deaf stare
as reflected in the mirror
as reflected in a photograph

the deaf stare is a dead giveaway

wherever I go and see another person,
I instantly can tell if he or she is deaf
by the deaf stare

one time at gymnastics meet,
I spot a guy my age.
naturally, my eyes take in his face,
then sliding over to his ears.
Yep, he is like me.

friends who are sitting with me,
lean over, "How can you tell?"
I point at my own face, "I know."

some do not realize it,
others are careful to not show it
or let down their guard

thus, I keep myself busy
wearing the green-striped sunflower dress,
letting the smile fill up my face,
erasing the deaf stare

thus, I keep myself busy
weaving the dandelions into wreaths,
transforming the deaf stare
into one of purpose and activity

nevertheless, the deaf stare
aligns with the concentration,
the focus of paying attention,
the listening face

I slowly circle back to accepting
the deaf stare, wearing it as
a wreath of dandelions,
wearing it as my favorite dress
of green-striped fabric with
a beautiful sunflower on it.

the innate sense of siblings

growing up with a sibling
with hearing impairment?

just like growing up
with a hearing sibling

yet growing up, perspective
adjusting to the realization of
having a different perspective,
yet wanting to be treated the same

no thought for special consideration,
never thinking anything
other than normal,
normal is the norm

when the sibling with hearing impairment
asked that cuing must stop,
her need for normal
persists

the persisting need pervades more,
the more the world outside the home
not giving the same treatment,
not giving the same interaction
not giving the same feedback

the sibling with hearing impairment
boomerangs to her siblings,
looking for cues of doing things right,
seeking validation of normal,
seeing is believing parallels siblings

yet faith without sight brings
more solidarity and solidness,
when surrounded by siblings
no frequent need for spoken assurance
only rare occasional need for verbal essence

no matter the societal interpretation,
siblings let being as being
no need to explain
no need to justify

the innate sense of siblings

no matter the societal interpretation,
siblings take in stride the questions
and comments, why no sign language?
because we did not grow up that way

siblings, the innate sense of siblings,
no expectations,
no special treatment,
no gods or idolization,
only normal as the norm
growing up with each other
as the sibling experience,
no less,
no more,
nothing special,
but special to the world
through the sibling bond
that no societal interpretation
can ever understand nor break

"You were our experience just like
we were your experience."

Hank, Brad, Sarah, Josie

writing to see | *Schrift zu sehen*

the spiral-bound notebook
from Mrs. Richburg's third grade,
along with Archie comics,
propel me through fourth grade
of reading Nancy Drew,
yearbook-influenced writing a play
about some high school drama,
thus grabbing the attention of
speech therapists who want to
see the connection between
writing and speaking

entering middle school,
reading more books to get that pizza,
co-penning with my soul sister Beth
the stories inspired by the thirteen ghosts
of Alabama, along with more journal writing,
learning some Spanish in history,
reading more and more, wanting
to immerse myself in worlds
where I get every word spoken,
while navigating the woes of
riding the bus, discovering boys,
and square dancing in PE

the AJHS campus where my father
first saw my mother walking
up the steps to the front door,
using the lockers for the first time,
my own space where I can control
by organizing my books and writing
utensils, along with a brush and mirror,
swapping football triangle notes
with friends back and forth,
            —much better than being left out of
            telephone social norms,
plunging into yearbook production,
journalism, and drama to give more
flavor to my writing while dealing
with the hormonal realities of
teenage angst, wearing big sneakers and
big "Cousin It" hair dwarfing my stick-thin legs

arriving at the high school,
my parents' alma mater,
my dark honey tresses carefully cherished,
a symbol of my feminineness and more so,
independence and desire for normal
            as I gaze at the
            upperclassmen with wonder,
writing in the journals, watching
my handwriting curve haphazard,
slanting and scrawling across paper
processing who I am while wanting

to be normal like my peers,
yet taking Deutsch instead of the popular
Spanish with their baking bread of the dead,
or French with no "s" pronunciation,

—*was sie sieht*, what she sees—

flipping through yearbook page layouts
with a ruler, double-checking picas,
measuring to crop black and white
photographs hastily developed
by peers in the darkroom due to
white hairlines or black splotches,

studying, copying notes, listening,
my eyes glazing over from listening,
my listening as lipreading,
my listening as watching the transliterator
all day long, waking up by looking away
and seeing the teacher up front, reviving
my listening energy

reading, writing, designing layouts
refueling with creativity and productivity
reaching out to peers through involvement
and leadership, smoothing over the ambivalence
of graduating and not knowing what to do,
entering the university, plunging back into
reading, writing, designing layouts

writing to explore what normal means
writing to expand my understanding
writing to express my voice

writing to see, *Schrift zu sehen*
see the writing, *die Schrift lesen*

9 789358 735604